C4013Q2436

*89* WORDS
followed by
PRAGUE, *A Disappearing Poem*

ALSO BY MILAN KUNDERA

FICTION
- *The Joke*
- *Laughable Loves*
- *Life Is Elsewhere*
- *Farewell Waltz*
- *The Book of Laughter and Forgetting*
- *The Unbearable Lightness of Being*
- *Immortality*
- *Slowness*
- *Identity*
- *Ignorance*
- *The Festival of Insignificance*

NONFICTION
- *A Kidnapped West*

Essays
- *The Art of the Novel*
- *Testaments Betrayed*
- *The Curtain*
- *Encounter*

Plays
- *Jacques and His Master*

# 89 WORDS

followed by

# PRAGUE, A Disappearing Poem

MILAN KUNDERA
Translated from the French by Matt Reeck

faber

This hardback edition first published in 2025
by Faber & Faber Limited
The Bindery, 51 Hatton Garden
London EC1N 8HN

First published in the United States in 2025
by HarperCollins Publishers
195 Broadway, New York, NY 10007

Typeset by Bonni Leon-Berman
Printed and bound by CPI Group (UK) Ltd, Croydon, CR0 4YY

All rights reserved
Copyright © 2023 by Éditions Gallimard–Estate Milan Kundera.
Translation copyright © Matt Reeck, 2025
by Éditions Gallimard–Estate Milan Kundera.

*89 Words* originally published as *Quatre-vingt-neuf mots* © 1985
by Milan Kundera. Originally published in French by Le Débat.

Excerpts from "Sixty-nine Words," *The Art of the Novel* originally
published as Extraits de « Soixante-neuf mots », *L'Art du roman* © 1986
by Milan Kundera.

*Prague, A Disappearing Poem* originally published as *Prague, poème qui
disparaît* © 1980 by Milan Kundera. Originally published in French
by Le Débat.

The right of Milan Kundera to be identified as author of this work
has been asserted in accordance with Section 77 of the Copyright,
Designs and Patents Act 1988

A CIP record for this book is available from the British Library

ISBN 978–0–571–39323–7

MIX
Paper | Supporting responsible forestry
FSC® C013604

Printed and bound in the UK on FSC® certified paper in line with our continuing
commitment to ethical business practices, sustainability and the environment.
**For further information see faber.co.uk/environmental-policy**

Our authorised representative in the EU for product safety is
Easy Access System Europe, Mustamäe tee 50, 10621 Tallinn, Estonia
gpsr.requests@easproject.com

2 4 6 8 10 9 7 5 3 1

## CONTENTS

Foreword by Pierre Nora | vii

89 Words | 1

Prague, A Disappearing Poem | 57

Other Books by Milan Kundera | 87

# FOREWORD

**These two texts originally appeared in *Le Débat*.**

"89 Words" was published in November 1985 as part of a series called "Words upon Words," edited by Michel Tournier; Kundera's essay was followed directly by "Little Dictionary of Creole Words and Birds" by J. M. G. Le Clézio. "Prague, A Disappearing Poem," appeared in June 1980, in the second issue of the magazine.

These are very personal texts. An intimate dictionary captures a personality's quintessence. This is especially true in the case of Milan Kundera, to the extent that this Czech writer would never see his books published in the language he had used to write them. Words were the object of his constant scrutiny. The importance to him of these words was made doubly clear when he included this list in his 1986 book *The Art of the Novel*,* reducing the list by about a third and sometimes modifying his commentary. A comparison of the two would be an interesting study. In *The Art of the Novel*, he also added twelve words that we have made sure to put

---

* Milan Kundera, *The Art of the Novel*, tr. Linda Asher (New York: Harper, 2003).

back into his original version and to highlight here with an asterisk.

As for "Prague, A Disappearing Poem," reading this emotional and excellent essay will show what it meant for him. This is the milieu from which Kundera emerged; it gives a behind-the-scenes look at the specificity of that culture: the richness of a culture born in a "small nation" but whose significance is universal. Here, as in *A Kidnapped West*,* we find the double condemnation of "Soviet civilization," which had suffocated and persecuted his culture, and of Western Europe, which couldn't find it in itself to acknowledge Kundera's culture, let alone understand it.

While Kundera has recently left us, the republication of these two texts under the same cover returns us to his living presence. Our intention, indeed our deepest wish, is that these texts will serve for some readers as the best introduction to Kundera's novels and, for others, a reminder of his keen sense of irony and subtle judgment.

—*Pierre Nora*

---

* Milan Kundera, *A Kidnapped West: The Tragedy of Central Europe*, tr. Linda Asher (New York: Harper, 2023).

*89 Words*
followed by
Prague, *A Disappearing Poem*

# 89 WORDS

for Pierre

In 1968 and 1969, *The Joke* was translated into all Western European languages. What a disaster! In France, the translator practically rewrote my novel and changed my style completely. In England, the publisher cut all the philosophical passages, eliminated all the musicological chapters, changed the order of its parts—in short, rewrote the novel. Then there was this in another country. I met my translator. He didn't know a single word of Czech. "How did you translate it?" I asked. "With my heart," he said. And he brought out a photo of me from his wallet. He was so nice that I almost believed it was possible to translate through telepathy and emotional intelligence. But the situation was simpler than that: he had performed bridge translation from the French translation, just like the Argentinian translator. In Spain, the novel was translated from Czech. I opened the book at random; it was Helena's monologue. My paragraph-long sentences are broken down into short sentences. I closed the cover. But did the punishment of these translations end with *The Joke*? Yes. In France, I found a translator and friend, François Kérel, whose faithful translations were wonderful. But I still had to spend way too much time correcting the English, German, and even Italian translations of my next novels. And often I got there too late to repair what needed to be repaired.

It's said that translation is like a woman: either beautiful or faithful. Say it's not so! An American translated *Jacques and His Master* (from the French, which I'd done myself). I read the manuscript. It was error after error. Then I understood. They weren't errors. The lack of faithfulness was *intended*. He wanted to make a good English book; he forced himself to forget that the text wasn't his; he tried to think, feel, and imagine in my place! To lighten the text, he added a word here and there, almost everywhere; he switched the order of my syntax systematically. I held myself to only correcting errors in meaning. If not, I would have had to rewrite the whole thing. . . . One year later, Simon Callow, the famous British actor, wanted to play Jacques, and he retranslated the text. Everyone agrees that his translation was a thousand times better than the first. And everyone thought, "The famous actor certainly gave himself a lot of freedom when it came to translating. That's why the dialogue is so rich and natural!" Not true! This translation is the most faithful of all my books.

A translation is beautiful only if it is faithful. It's the passion for faithfulness that makes an authentic translator! With this in mind, I decided some years ago to put right the foreign editions of my books. It wasn't easy. I had to leave many publishers for others who still took literature seriously: Claude Gallimard, Aaron Asher, Kathryn Court, Roberto Calasso, Christoph Schlotterer, Robert McCrum, Ivo Gay, and Beatriz de Moura. They helped me, and I'm grateful. This was how I was able to revise (with Claude Courtot) the first French translation of *The Joke*, and new translations of this novel began to appear in the US, Britain, and Spain, with Italy and Germany to follow. The revised translation of *Life Is Elsewhere* came out in the US this year. Hanser Verlag released revised editions of all my novels. And I hope that Adelphi will be able to do the same thing.

What is for certain is that there's no other author so sick of translations as me. It's not that other authors are better translated than me, but they aren't as affected by the translated versions of their books. Before the Russian invasion in 1968, *The Joke* and *Laughable Loves* were published in Prague. Since I had Czech readers, I hardly bothered with a foreign audience. But, after 1968, my other novels couldn't get published in Czechoslovakia, and they appeared in their original language only through a tiny publisher in Canada that published hardly any copies at all. I was imagining that at least a couple of copies could get into my old country. But the border was almost impenetrable. Even my closest friends in Prague had never seen a single Czech version of my books.

So I was writing my Czech novels for whom exactly? For a handful of my exiled countryfolk. For a chain of university libraries. And for translators. Yes. But as the country grew more and more ensconced in Russian rule, interest in the Czech language weakened everywhere. For the most part, my translators are Slavicists for whom Czech is only a third or fourth language. Many foreign publishers ask me to translate first into French. I refuse out of principle. But what if there are no Czech translators in their countries?

While I was writing *The Unbearable Lightness of Being*, Prague was strong on my mind, but were my Czech readers? The only person I could definitively say I was thinking about was François Kérel, who was going to translate my manuscript. I formulated my sentences while already listening, as in echo, to their future French versions. And because I closely supervised the translation work, I no longer saw any difference from the original. And I could even let it be translated (in Portugal, Brazil, Greece, Sweden, Iceland, and Norway) from the French version, which I had put my weight behind.

For a number of years now, I have tried my hand at writing articles and essays in French. But thinking and storytelling are two different things: I feel that writing a novel in French would be impossible. However, I can't stop myself from reading the French versions of my books as though they were entirely my own. Still, the corrections I introduced into the French translation of *The Joke* in 1980 seemed not enough, and so I took up the work again, from beginning to end, and I have reread the new editions of all my texts in French translation, and I can finally say that they have the same mark of authenticity as the original Czech.

Then, one day, Pierre Nora said to me, "Reading through all the translations of your work out there, you must have turned over each and every word in your mind. Why don't you write a personal dictionary? Keywords, words you get hung up on, words you love? . . ." The idea lit a fire under me. It was all but done.

———

**ABSOLUTE.** As a form, the novel touches on the metaphysical, and so metaphysical words (the "absolute," "essence," "being," etc.) find their natural setting in the novel. But in the novel they must be protected against the vulgarization of spoken language. It's unacceptable to say "absolutely" instead of "completely," "essential" instead of "important," and "absurd" instead of "stupid."

**AMUSING.** It's good to *be* amusing, it's less good to *force* things to be funny. The French translator of *The Joke* writes: "She had lived through nineteen springs" (instead of "she was nineteen years old"); "They were wearing Eve costumes" (instead of "were nude"); "The harmonium emitted grumbling noises" (instead of "sounds"). The American translator has the same desire to be funny. Aaron Asher, my publisher and close friend, reads the proofs with a heightened attention. He phones me, "I'm getting rid of all the *amusing* words!"

**APHORISM.** From the Greek word *aphorismos*, which means "definition." An aphorism: the poetic form of a definition.

**AROUSAL.** Not pleasure, jouissance, feeling, or passion. Arousal is the basis of eroticism, its most profound riddle, its key word. "Jan told himself: at the beginning of man's erotic life, there's arousal without jouissance, and, at the end, jouissance without arousal" (*The Book of Laughter and Forgetting*).

**AT-HOME.** "The home" (in English), "*das Heim*" (in German), "*domov*" (in Czech): the place where I have my roots, where I belong. The topographical limits are determined only by the heart's decree: it can be a single room, a landscape, a country, a universe. "*Das Heim*" is from classical German philosophy: the ancient Greek world. The Czech national anthem begins with the line, "Where is my *domov*?" Or, in French, "Where is my motherland?" But the motherland is something else: the political, national version of "*domov*." "Motherland," a proud word. "*Das Heim*," a sentimental word. Between motherland and living room (my own particular home), there is a lacuna in French (or in French sensibility). The only way to cover it over is to make "at-home" into an important word. (See **LITANY**.)

★ BEAUTY (and KNOWLEDGE). Those who say, along with Broch, that knowledge is the novel's only moral end are betrayed by the metallic aura of the word "knowledge," which is compromised by its connections to science. More is needed: the novel discovers every aspect of existence, including beauty. The first novelists discovered adventure. It's thanks to them that adventure seems beautiful and something we want. Kafka described the situation of a person who is tragically trapped. Those who study Kafka used to argue a lot about whether the author was giving us any hope or not. No, no hope. Something else. But Kafka discovers how the unlivable situation is both strange and full of black beauty. Beauty: the last possible victory of a person who has lost hope. Beauty in art: the light subtly emanating from the never-said. This light suffuses great novels; there will never be a time when it fades because, human existence being perpetually forgotten by people, the discoveries of novelists, even when they become dated, will never cease to amaze us.


BEING. Many friends advised me not to call the book *The Unbearable Lightness of Being*. Couldn't I at least get rid of the word "being"? The word embarrasses everyone. Translators tend to replace it with more modest words: "existence," "life," "condition." . . . A Czech translator wanted to modernize *Hamlet*: "To live or not to live . . ." But it's precisely there, in that famous monologue, where the difference between life and being is revealed: If, after death, we continue to dream, if after death there *is* still something, then death (non-life) doesn't rid us of the horror of being. Hamlet asks the question of being, not of life. The horror of being: "Death has two faces. Non-being. And being, the terrifyingly material being of the corpse" (*The Book of Laughter and Forgetting*).

BETRAYAL. "But what does betrayal mean? Betrayal means breaking ranks. Betrayal means breaking ranks and setting off into the unknown. Sabina knew of nothing more beautiful than setting off into the unknown" (*The Unbearable Lightness of Being*).

BLUISH. No other color captures this linguistic form of tenderness. This Novalis-like word. "Like non-being, death—tender and bluish."

BOOK. If I've heard it said once, I've heard it said a thousand times on various radio broadcasts: "As I say in my *book* . . ."

The word "book" is given such weight, it's stretched out

so long and pronounced at least an octave above all the other words. When the same person says, "As people in my town say . . ." there's no special emphasis on the word "town," which has almost the same intonation. *"My book"* . . . the phonetic cue for literary masturbation.

**BORDER.** "So little is needed, so very little, to find yourself on the other side of the border where nothing makes sense: love, convictions, faith, history. All the mystery of human life stems from the fact that it takes place so very close to this border, even in direct contact with it, that it's not separated by kilometers, but hardly even a millimeter. . . ." (*The Book of Laughter and Forgetting*).

**CACHE** (to cache). Maybe the charm of this verb for me is that I imagine another word in it: to "seal." To cache = to seal, though without a seal; to hide while sealing; to seal in order to preserve.

★ **CENTRAL EUROPE.** Seventeenth century: The immense power of the Baroque gave a certain cultural unity to this multinational region without a clear center, with moving and indefinable borders. The lingering shadow of Baroque

Catholicism extended into the eighteenth century: no Voltaire, no Fielding. In the hierarchy of the arts, it was music that rose to the top. Since Haydn (and until Schoenberg and Bartók), this was the gravitational center for European music. Nineteenth century: some master poets, but no Flaubert; Biedermeier: the veil of the idyll thrown over the real. In the twentieth century, revolt. The great minds (Freud, the novelists) revalorized what had been unknown, misunderstood, for centuries: rational, demystifying lucidity; the meaning of the real; the novel. Their revolt was exactly the opposite of French modernism—it was antirational, antirealist, lyrical. (This would cause many misunderstandings.) The Mount Rushmore of the greatest Central European novelists includes Kafka, Hašek, Musil, Broch, and Gombrowicz, who are united in their aversion to Romanticism; their love for the pre-Balzacian novel and for the libertine spirit (Broch interpreted kitsch as a conspiracy of monogamous Puritans against the Enlightenment); their disregard for History and their exaltation of the future; and their modernism that lay outside the illusions of the avant-garde.

The destruction of the empire followed by the cultural marginalization of Austria and the political nonexistence of its other countries after 1945 made Central Europe into a premonition, a mirror held up to the possible destiny of Europe, the laboratory of the crepuscule.

★ **CENTRAL EUROPE** (and **EUROPE**). In the blurb, the publisher wants to situate Broch in a steadfastly Central European context: Hofmannsthal, Svevo. Broch won't stand for it. If they want to compare him to someone, then why not Gide or Joyce? Does he want to renounce his "Central Europeanness"? No, he only wanted to say that national and regional contexts do nothing when it comes to capturing the meaning and worth of an oeuvre.

**CHARACTERS.** Characters are shrinking in today's novels. I threw away Tibor Déry's *The Unfinished Sentence*. Unreadable. Joseph Roth's *Radetzky March* in paperback: unreadable. I imagine literature's death: little by little, without anyone realizing it, characters will become so small that they're completely invisible.

**COATRACK.** Another magical object. Ludvik sees one while looking for Helena. He imagines she's committed suicide: "The metal stand, rising from three feet, spread out at its top into three branches; it held no garments to speak of; it seemed orphaned in its vaguely human form; its metallic nudity and its ridiculously raised arms filled me with anguish." Later on: "A metal, skinny coatrack that raised its arms like a surrendering soldier." I dreamed of putting on the cover of

*The Joke* an image of this object that brings to life for me the novel's atmosphere.

**COLLABO.** In new historical circumstances, we are confronted by the timeless limits of human possibility, which we're asked to name. So the word "collaboration" took on a new sense after the war against the Nazis: to be voluntarily in the service of a corrupt power. What a basic notion! How could humanity have lacked this word up to 1944? Once the word is discovered, it's possible to identify the human activity of collaboration. All those in love with the brouhaha of mass media, the imbecilic smile of advertising, the destruction of nature, indiscretion raised to the status of a virtue, these are called "collabos of modernity."

**COMIC.** In offering us a beautiful illusion of human greatness, tragedy brings with it this one consolation. Comedy is crueler: it reveals to us in brutal terms the meaninglessness of everything. I guess that everything human has its comic side that, in certain cases, is widely known, admitted, exploited, and, in other cases, hidden from view. The true comic geniuses aren't those who make us laugh the most but those who use comedy to reveal the *unknown*. History was also considered an exclusively serious terrain. However, there's the unknown comic side of History. Just as there's the comic side of sexuality (which is difficult to accept). (Here, homage to two friends: Philip Roth and Miloš Forman—to his *Firemen's Ball*, in particular.)

**CREPUSCULE** (and **VELOCIPEDIST**). "Velocipedist (this word felt to him as beautiful as crepuscule) . . ." (*Life Is Elsewhere*). These two nouns are magical to me because they come from so far away. *Crepusculum*, one of Ovid's beloved words. "Velocipede," a word that comes to us from the distant and naïve beginnings of the Industrial Age.

**CZECHOSLOVAKIA.** I never use the word "Czechoslovakia" in my novels, even though they're mostly set there. This compound word is too young (born in 1918), it doesn't have roots stretching back in time, it's without beauty, and it betrays the cobbled-together and absurdly young character (untested by time) of what it attempts to name. While it's possible to create a nation on the basis of such a flimsy word (and to do so intentionally), you can't write a novel about it. That's why I always use "Bohemia," the old word for it. In terms of political geography, it's not really right (my translators flip out about it, from time to time), but from a poetic point of view, it's the only choice.

**DEFINITION.** The meditative dimension of a novel is sustained by the armature of several abstract words. If I don't want to fall prey to the pitfall where everyone thinks they understand everything without understanding anything, it's important for me not only to choose my words with extreme precision but to define them and redefine them. (See: **BETRAYAL, BORDER, DUMB, LIGHTNESS, LYRICISM, PARADISE.**) Often a novel is nothing but a long pursuit of several difficult-to-capture definitions. Or so it seems to me.

**DESTINY.** It arrives the moment when the image of our life separates from our life itself, becomes independent, and, little by little, begins to dominate us. Already in *The Joke*: "There was no means for me to rectify the image of my person, set within the enormous courtroom of human destinies; I understood that this image (however little it resembled me) was infinitely more real than myself; that it was definitely not my shadow, but that I was, *I was*, the shadow of my image; that it wasn't possible in any way, shape, or form to accuse it of not resembling me, but that I was the one guilty of dissembling."

And in *The Book of Laughter and Forgetting*: "That's how, if you ask me, life changes into destiny. Destiny wasn't about to lift even its pinkie for Mirek (for his beauty, his security, his good mood, and his health), while Mirek was ready to do everything for his destiny (for its grandeur, clarity, style, and intelligibility). He felt responsible for his destiny, but his destiny didn't feel responsible for him."

Unlike Mirek, the hedonistic fortysomething in *Life Is Elsewhere* holds to "the idyll of his non-destiny." In sum, the hedonist defends himself against the transformation of his life into destiny. Destiny preys on us, like a vampire; it weighs us down, it's like an iron ball on a chain that we drag behind us. (The fortysomething, just to let you know, most resembled me, out of all my characters.)

**DUMB.** "About a year before my dad's death, we were taking our normal walk. . . . The sadder people got, the more the loudspeakers counted for them. . . . Dad stopped, he looked up, toward the loudspeaker and its noise, and I felt that he wanted to tell me something very important. Slowly, and painfully, he said: 'Music's so dumb!'" (*The Book of Laughter and Forgetting*).

In the first French edition, Kérel and I opted for "the idiocy of music!" But "idiocy" is an aggressive, emotional, injurious word. It's better to say "dumb." That's exactly what I mean, as explained by the narrator directly following my father's exclamation: "I think he wanted to tell me that there was an original form of music, before its own history started, before anyone had ever questioned it, or thought about it, before the first setting of motif and theme. There, in that first state of music (music before thought) we can find the inherent stupidity of the human condition."

There are languages where the word "dumb" is translatable only by "aggressive" words: "cretin," "stupid," "imbecilic," etc. As though being dumb were something exceptional, a shortcoming, an abnormality, and not our "inherent human condition."


**EIGHTY-NINE.** Prime numbers. They're solid, like a fortress: indivisible, indestructible. The ideal mathematical base for a work's architecture. As for the number itself, the numbers 8 and 9 give it the charm of a couple of Swedish athletes, tall and lean. To be beautiful like 89. The magical number of the alchemists in Rudolf II's court.


**ELITISM.** The word "elitism" appeared in France in 1967. The word "elitist" in 1968. For the first time in history, the French language cast a bright shining light of negativity, even scorn, upon the notion of the elite.

Official propaganda in Communist countries began to lambaste elitism and the elites in the same years. Through the words "elitism" and "elite," this propaganda took aim not at CEOs, popular sports players, or politicians but exclusively at the cultural elite: philosophers, writers, professors, historians, filmmakers, and theater directors.

A stunning synchronicity. It makes you think that all over Europe one cultural elite is being replaced by others. A police elite there. A mass media elite here. No one will accuse these new elites of elitism. And the word "elitism" will fall out of use, forgotten.

★ EUROPE. During the Middle Ages, European unity was based on a common religion. In the modern era, religion ceded place to culture (art, literature, philosophy), which became the realization of the highest values through which Europeans recognized themselves, defined themselves, and of which they were proud. However, today, culture has been left behind. But to what, and to whom? Where will the loftiest values capable of uniting Europe coalesce? Technology? Economics? The democratic ideal in politics, the principle of tolerance? But will this tolerance be empty and useless if it doesn't protect exalted creativity or strong thinking? Or can we consider the jettisoning of culture as an act of deliverance that we should welcome with open arms? I don't know. I only know that culture has already been pushed aside. And with it, the image of a European identity recedes into the past. European: a person nostalgic for Europe.

**FLOW.** In a letter, Chopin describes his trip to England. He plays in salons, and ladies always wax eloquent, using the same phrase, "Oh, how beautiful! It flows like water!" This got under Chopin's skin, just like it does mine when I hear anyone lavish praise on a translation by saying, "It flows well." Or even: "You might say it was written by a French writer!" But it would be very bad if Hemingway was a French writer! "If it's a good translation, it must be clear that it's a translation!" François Kérel said, against popular opinion.

**FORGETTING.** "The struggle of man against power is the struggle of the memory against forgetting." This is an indirect quote from Mirek in *The Book of Laughter and Forgetting*, and this line is often quoted as if it were the novel's message. What's really happening is that a novel makes the reader think of something familiar. In this case, it's the famous Orwellian theme: the forgetting imposed by a totalitarian regime. But the originality of my novel about Mirek is something else entirely. It's how Mirek works tirelessly so that we don't forget him (him and his friends and their political struggle), while at the same time he moves mountains to make us forget someone else (his mistress, whom he's ashamed of). Before becoming a political problem, the desire for forgetting is first an anthropological problem: from time immemorial, people have always had the desire to rewrite their own biographies, to change the past, to erase its traces, both their own traces and those of others. The desire to forget things is far from being a simple temptation to cheat. Sabina in *The Unbearable Lightness of Being* had no reason to hide anything, and yet she is obsessed with an irrational desire to forget herself. Forgetting: absolute injustice and absolute consolation at the same time. The study of this theme in novels is endless, and it lacks a conclusion.

**FORNICATE.** In *Laughable Loves*, Alice wants to believe in God and obey his commandments. Yet there is one commandment that seems far from self-evident to her, and it represents a challenge: no sex outside of marriage! So, for her, God shrinks into a non-fucking God ("*Bůh nesouloze*"). In French: God, the Anti-Fucker.

**FORSAKEN.** Thrown, thrust into solitude. The most expressive word of its class: solitary, abandoned, alone, etc. It brings up the image of a weeping willow.

**GET HARD** (to get a hard-on). "His body ended its passive resistance; Édouard was piqued!" This time, I paused, unhappy about the word "piqued." In Czech, Édouard is "excited." But neither "piqued" nor "excited" was satisfying. Then, suddenly, I thought of it! I needed to say, "Édouard got a hard-on!" Why hadn't this simple idea come to me earlier? Because the word doesn't exist in Czech. Oh, what a shame! My mother tongue doesn't know how to get a hard-on! Instead of saying he "got a hard-on," Czechs have to say: "his dick stood up." A charming image, but a bit childish. Still, there's a very nice saying that comes from this phrase: "They were standing there like a bunch of stiff dicks."


**GRAPHOMANIA.** It isn't "the mania for writing letters, personal diaries, family chronicles (in other words, to write for yourself and those close to you), but for writing books (so to have an audience of unknown readers)" (*The Book of Laughter and Forgetting*). It's a common word in Prague. But in France, it's hardly ever used. How is that possible? Answer: if a mania is shared by all, it's hard to make it out. It's not even a mania; it's part of the essence of the country.


**HAGGARD.** I love this old German word, which expresses the feeling of being lost in a foreign language.

**HAT.** Every novelist has those "magical objects" that always keep coming back. In *The Book of Laughter and Forgetting*, a hat fell into the grave and rested on the coffin "as though the dead person, in a vain desire to maintain dignity, hadn't wanted to remain without a hat on during the solemn occasion." A bowler hat is everywhere in *The Unbearable Lightness of Being*. I remember a dream: A ten-year-old boy is next to a pond, with a large black hat on. He jumps into the water. He's later pulled out, drowned. He still has the same black hat on, and in the dream I hear the words, "A black hat made out of rubber."


★ **IDEAS.** The disgust that I feel for those who reduce a literary work to its ideas. The horror that I feel for being led into what is called the "debate of ideas." The despair that the times cause in me due to their obsession with ideas and their indifference to literary works.


**IDYLL.** The state of the world before the first conflict; or outside of all conflicts; or with conflicts that are only misunderstandings, and so not true conflicts. "Even though he enjoyed a colorful erotic life, the middle-aged man was basically of an idyllic temperament. . . ." (*Life Is Elsewhere*).

The desire of merging the erotic adventure and the idyll is the very essence of hedonism and its impossibility.


★ IMAGINATION. "What did you mean to say through the story of Tamina on the island of children?" they asked me. This story was first a dream that fascinated me, which I then daydreamed about, then enlarged and deepened while writing. Its meaning? If you must ask: a dream song of a world ruled by children. (See: **INFANTOCRACY**.) Yet this meaning didn't precede the dream; it's the dream that came before the meaning. So you have to read this story while letting your imagination lead you along. God forbid, it's not a puzzle to solve. It's in trying to decipher Kafka that Kafka scholars kill Kafka.


INEXPERIENCE. The provisional title for *The Unbearable Lightness of Being* was *The Planet of Inexperience*. Inexperience, which characterizes the human condition. We're born just once; we don't get a do-over in which we can use the experiences of our past life. We grow out of childhood not knowing what it means to be a teen. We get married not knowing what it means to be married, and even when we grow old, no one knows where that will take us: the old are like children in their ignorance about their age. So, we inhabit the "planet of inexperience."

★ **INFANTOCRACY.** "A motorcyclist sped down the empty street, arms and legs molded into an O, and then came back up in a clap of thunder; his face glistening with the self-important air of a screaming child" (Musil in *The Man Without Qualities*). A self-important air: the face of the technological. Infantocracy: the ideal of childhood imposed on humanity.

**INTERVIEW.** Curses on the first writer who allowed a journalist to quote him off the cuff! He started the process that would lead directly to the disappearance of the writer: the person who is responsible for each word. However, I really like *dialogue* (a major literary form), and I was pleased to help publish some redesigned and rewritten interviews I'd done. Yet an interview, such as it is normally conducted, has nothing in common with dialogue: (1) the interviewer asks questions that interest them, but not you; (2) only the answers that work for the interviewer are used; (3) the interviewer translates them into new words to fit their way of thinking. Led on by American journalism, the interviewer doesn't even bother showing you what he's going to quote you as having said. The interview appears. You console yourself: Everyone will forget about it soon enough! But not at all: It's going to get cited! Not even the most scrupulous professor notices the difference between words that a writer has written and signed off on and secondhand statements.

In June 1985, I had had my fill: no more interviews. Only dialogues, coedited by me, *under my copyright*. From that date forward, anything else reported by journalists must be assumed to be false.

**IRONY.** Which character is right, and which, wrong? Is Emma Bovary a pain in the ass? Or is she courageous, inspiring? No answer. The novel is by its very nature ironic, by which I mean its "truth" is hidden, unpronounced and unpronounceable. People want simplified portraits of the world where good and bad are clearly separated. With the heroism of Don Quixote, the novel finds itself in this inalterable terrain, while revealing to us the fundamental ambiguity of human affairs. Irony isn't a personal penchant of this or that writer. It's the essence of the novel as an art form. Irony = the way of making the ambiguous known.

**KITSCH.** When I wrote *The Unbearable Lightness of Being*, I was a little worried about having made the word "kitsch" one of the pillars of the novel. Indeed, until just recently, the word was hardly known in France, or known, but as a shell of itself. In the French version of the famous essay by Hermann Broch, the word "kitsch" is translated as "the art of junk." This is not what it means. Because Broch demonstrates that kitsch is something other than artwork made in bad taste. There's a kitsch attitude. A kitsch comportment. The need that the kitsch man (*"Kitsch-mensch"*) feels is the need to see himself in the mirror of the embellishing lie and to recognize himself there with a pointed satisfaction. For Broch, kitsch is historically linked to the sentimental Romanticism of the nineteenth century. Because the nineteenth century in Germany and in Central Europe was more Romantic than elsewhere (and less realist), the word "kitsch" was born there, and is used there in profusion up till today. In Prague, modern artists always saw in kitsch the basis of an aesthetics of perversion. In France, it's too light to be considered art. A minor art, not a good art. As for myself, I've never had any bad reaction to Belmondo's cop flicks! I love them! They're honest, they don't have any pretense! By contrast, Tchaikovsky's piano concerto, the mawkish Rachmaninoff, the big Hollywood films, *Kramer vs. Kramer*, *Doctor Zhivago* (O poor Pasternak!)—these are what I hate, deeply, and with all sincerity. And I'm more and more irritated by the spirit of kitsch that is *present* in works that try to be modernist. (Note: Nietzsche's aversion to the "beautiful language" and the "grand spectacles" in Victor Hugo and the "inimitable saccharinity" of Richard Wagner was disgust brought on by kitsch before it was even a thing to feel that way.)

**LAUGH** (European). For Rabelais, happiness and comedy weren't the same thing. In the eighteenth century, the humor of Sterne and Diderot is a tender and nostalgic memory of the humor of Rabelais. In the nineteenth century, Gogol is a melancholic humor writer. "When we pay consistent attention to a funny story, it gets sadder and sadder," he once said. Europe has looked back on the comic story of its own existence for so long that, by the twentieth century, Rabelais's comic epics have ceded ground to Ionesco's despairing fare. "There's little that separates the horrible from the comic," Ionesco said. The history of European comedy, blow by blow.

**LAZINESS** (*oisiveté*). The mother of all vices. Too bad that in French this word sounds so good it becomes seductive. It's because of the resonance of another word: the summer bird *oiseau d'été* becomes *oisiveté*.

**LIFE** (with a capital *L*). Paul Éluard, in the surrealist pamphlet *A Corpse*, addresses the freshly deceased Anatole France: "Corpse, we don't like those who are like you. . . ." After kicking the dead man's coffin, he justified it in this way: "Life, which I can no longer think about without tears coming to my eyes, appears even today in the little negligible things that only tenderness can now maintain. Skepticism, irony, cowardice, France, the French spirit—what does any of it mean? A big gust of forgetfulness takes me far away from all of that. Could it be that I never read about what dishonors Life, and never heard tell of it, either?"

Set off against skepticism and irony were negligible things, tears in the eyes, tenderness, the honor of Life, yes, life with a capital *L*! A stiff kick to the coffin, all in the name of the flattest sort of kitsch!

**LIGHTNESS.** As for the idea of the unbearable lightness of being, I find it already in *The Joke*: "I was walking across the dusty cobblestones, and I felt the heavy lightness that weighed down my life."

And in *Life Is Elsewhere*: "Jaromil sometimes had terrifying dreams: he dreamed that he had to pick up an extremely light object—a teacup, a spoon, a feather—and that he couldn't; that he grew increasingly weak as the object got lighter, that he collapsed beneath its lightness."

And in *The Farewell Waltz*: "Raskolnikov experienced his crime as a tragedy and in the end he collapsed beneath the weight of his act. And Jakub was amazed that his act was so light, that it didn't weigh him down, that it weighed nothing. And he wondered if this lightness wasn't as terrifying as the Russian character's hysterics."

And in *The Book of Laughter and Forgetting*: "The hollow

feeling in the stomach is simply the unbearable absence of weight. And in just the same way that one extreme can at any moment turn into its opposite, this lightness, carried to its extreme, has become the terrifying heaviness of lightness, and Tamina knows that she won't be able to withstand it for one second longer."

It was only in going over my translations that I saw, in horror, these repetitions! Then I consoled myself: it might be that novelists end up writing the same novel over and over—the first novel, and its *variations*.

**LITANY.** Repetition: a principle of musical composition. Litany: words become music. I want the novel to become a song in its self-reflective passages. Here's a passage composed through litany in *The Joke* on the phrase "at home": "And it came to me that I was born from within these songs, they had fashioned me, they were *my home*, which I had betrayed, but it was still my home (since the most poignant complaint comes from the home betrayed); but I understood at the same time that this home wasn't of this world (but what home was it, if it wasn't of this world?), that everything we sang about was only a memory, a monument, an imaginary collection of what no longer existed, and I felt the floor of my home give way beneath my feet and I slipped, with the clarinet on my lips, into the depth of years, centuries, into a bottomless pit, and I told myself, shocked, that my only home was in fact this descent, this avid and grasping fall, and I was abandoning myself to it and to the voluptuousness of my vertigo."

In the first French translation, before I had the chance to correct it, all the repetitions were replaced by synonyms: "And it seemed to me that inside these couplets, I was at home, that I had come from them, that their entity was my original sign, my foyer which, for having wiped clean my departure, still belonging to me nevertheless (since the most poignant complaint comes from the nest that we have let down); it's true that as a prodigal son I understood that it wasn't of this world (but what resthouse could it be about, if it wasn't in the here-below?), that the flesh of our songs and our melodies had no other weight than that of memory, monument, imagined afterlife of the fabulous real that no longer existed, and I felt from under my feet the continental shelf of this foyer give way, I felt myself slip, with the clarinet on my lips, into the abyss without end and I said to myself, thoroughly shocked, that this descent was my only refuge, this avid and grasping fall, and so I fell fully into the voluptuousness of my vertigo."

**LYRIC.** In *The Unbearable Lightness of Being*, there are two types of men who chase after women: the lyric ones (who chase after their ideal) and the epic ones (who are smitten by the infinite diversity of women). This is based on the classical distinction of the lyric and the epic (and the dramatic), which appeared at the end of the eighteenth century in Germany and was developed in stunning fashion in Hegel's *Aesthetics*: The lyric is the expression of the confessing subject; the epic comes from the passion to touch the world's objectivity. For me, the lyric and the epic go beyond the aesthetic; they represent two possible attitudes for a person to have in regard to the self, the world, and others (the lyric age = youth). Yet this idea of the lyric and the epic was so unfamiliar to the French that I had to agree, for the French translation, to make the lyric into the romantic, and the epic into the libertine. It was the best solution, but I regretted having had to make it.

**LYRICISM** (and revolution). "Lyricism is drunkenness, and we get drunk to dive more easily into the world. The revolution doesn't want to be studied or observed, it wants to be united, body to body; this is what it means to be lyrical, and why lyricism is necessary for it" (*Life Is Elsewhere*). "The wall, behind which men and women were imprisoned, was papered over with poetry and, in front of this wall, people were dancing. No, not a danse macabre. Innocence was dancing! Innocence with its bloody smile" (*Life Is Elsewhere*).

**MACHO MAN.** The macho man loves women, and he wants to dominate what he adores. Through exalting the archetypal femininity of the dominated woman (her maternity, her fecundity, her weakness, her homeyness, her sentimentality, etc.), he exalts his own virility. In contrast, the misogynist hates femininity; he flees from women who are too womanly. The macho man's perfect world: the family. The misogynist's perfect world: being single with a lot of lovers; or married to a woman he loves, but with no kids.

**MEDIOCRITY.** This means first and foremost the quality of things that are in the middle, average. Then, its connotative meaning: what is worse than average, and so what is bad. The French language has lost an irreplaceable way of understanding the contemporary world: the notion of being average.

**MEDITATION.** The novelist's three basic possibilities: to *tell* a story (Fielding), to *describe* a story (Flaubert), to *conjure* a story (Musil). Novelistic description in the nineteenth century was in harmony with the spirit of the times (positivist, scientific). To write a novel that is a meditation goes against the spirit of the twentieth century, which hates to think.

**MERCI.** Why does this word sound so harsh in French? It's convincing only when ironically stated. You annoy someone; they say, "*Merci*." But then the word inspires this turn of phrase: to be at someone's mercy. To throw yourself on someone's mercy.

**MESSAGE.** Five years ago, the Scandinavian translator of *The Farewell Waltz* told me how the publishers had had grave doubts before publishing the book: "Everyone is on the Left here. Your message isn't for them.—And what is your message?—Isn't it an anti-abortion novel?" Of course not! In my heart of hearts, not only am I for abortion, I advocate for mandatory abortion! But I was tickled by this misunderstanding. I'd succeeded as a novelist. I'd succeeded in maintaining the moral ambiguity of the situation. I was faithful to the novel's artistic essence: irony. And irony hates messages!

**METAPHOR.** Highly regrettable when used as ornamentation, as an embellishment for style. But irreplaceable when used as a means of capturing, in an epiphany, the elusive nature of things, situations, people. Mrs. Hentjen and Esch make love: "His seeking mouth had found hers, that was now pressed against his like the muzzle of an animal against a pane of glass, and Esch was enraged because she kept her soul tightly enclosed behind her set teeth. . . ." Here is Esch's existentialism on display: "He wanted to create a world so strong in its simplicity that his own loneliness could be bound fast to it as to an iron stake."[*]

**MISOGYNIST.** From our earliest days, we are brought face-to-face with a mother and a father, with femininity and virility. We're shaped by the harmonious and disharmonious relation of these two archetypes. Gynophobes (misogynists) have a sense of identity that is not just masculine but is also feminine; and there are just as many misogynists as androgynists (those who aren't at home in the male archetype). These are different, legitimate reactions to the human condition. Feminist Manicheanism never sought to question androphobia and so transformed misogyny into a rude insult. So I've outlined the psychological profile of this notion, which is the only one that deserves further study.

**MISOMUSE.** A person who doesn't get art, which isn't a big deal. It's possible to never read Proust, never hear Schubert, and live happily. But the misomuse can't. Misomuses feel

---

[*] Hermann Broch, *The Sleep-Walkers*, tr. Willa and Edwin Muir (New York: Pantheon, 1947; San Francisco: North Point, 1985), 255, 539.

humiliated before art, which goes completely over their heads; they hate it. There is a general misomusia, just like there is a general anti-Semitism, in society. Fascist and Communist governments knew when to put it to good use when they were censuring modern art. But there is also intellectual misomusia, which is very sophisticated: Intellectuals take revenge on art by asking it to be something more than aesthetic. This is the platform of socially engaged art: art as a political operative. There are also professors who take an artwork in hand only to subject it to their methodological fantasies (psychoanalytic, semiological, sociological, etc.). Art's apocalypse: misomuses will turn to art, and their revenge will be complete.

**MODERN** (modern art, the modern world). There's modern art that, with a *lyric* ecstasy, is identified with the modern world. Apollinaire. The exaltation of technology, the fascination with the future. With and after him: Mayakovski, Léger, the futurists, all the avant-gardes. But against Apollinaire, there's Kafka. The modern world as a labyrinth where we get lost. *Antilyric* modernism that is unromantic, skeptical, and critical. With and after him: Musil, Broch, Gombrowicz, Beckett, Ionesco, Fellini. As we step further into the future, the heritage of antimodern modernism becomes richer.

**MODERN** (to be modern). "New, new, new is the star of Communism, outside of which there is no modernity," wrote the great Czech avant-garde novelist Vladislav Vancura around 1920. Everyone in his time ran to the Communist Party to be modern. The historical decline of the Communist Party was sealed as soon as it found itself everywhere "outside of modernity." Because, as Rimbaud commanded, "It's necessary to be absolutely modern." The desire to be modern is an archetype, that's to say, an irrational imperative, profoundly anchored in us, an insistent form whose contents are changing and not specific: being modern is declaring yourself modern and being accepted as modern. Mrs. Youngblood in *Ferdydurke* shows one way of being modern in "what had thus far been a covert activity—her now overt visits to the toilet."[*] Gombrowicz's *Ferdydurke*: the most hilarious send-up of the modern archetype.


**MODERN TIMES.** The coming of modern times. The divisive moment in European history. God became *Deus absconditus*, and people became the basis of everything. European individualism was born and with it a new art situation, also, a new cultural situation, and a new science situation. I see how difficult this phrase is to translate in America. If we write "modern times," Americans think we

---

[*] Witold Gombrowicz, *Ferdydurke*, 1938, tr. Danuta Borchardt (New Haven: Yale University Press, 2000), 134.

mean the contemporary world, our century. American ignorance about modern times reveals the gaping difference between the two continents. In Europe, we live at the end of modern times; the end of individualism; the end of art conceived of as being the expression of a personal, irreplaceable originality; the end announcing the birth of a new era of suffocating conformity. Americans don't feel this sense of endings because they didn't witness the birth of modern times, and they are only their belated heirs. Americans think of other things as being the beginning and end of times.

**MYSTIFICATION.** A ludic neologism, born in the eighteenth century. Diderot was forty-seven when he staged an extraordinary prank making the Marquis of Croismare believe that a young nun needed his protection. For months on end, he wrote letters signed by this fictional woman to the worried Marquis. *The Nun*—the fruit of mystification: yet another reason to like Diderot and his time. Mystification: the active means of not taking the world too seriously. This is the principal theme of *Laughable Loves*.

**NO MORE.** Words that mark the past. "Once" is neutral. "Formerly" sounds to me like a medical verdict. "No more"— a plaint. But maybe it's my Czech accent that makes it so stunningly plaintive in its marking lost time. No more. No *moorrrre*!


**NON-.** In Czech or in German, there are almost unlimited possibilities of creating negative nouns by a simple prefix. "*Die Unwelt*," coined by Heidegger: the non-world; the un-world; the world stripped of its essence. Or in the poetry of Vladimir Holan: "There is the unleafed in the leafed." To translate these into French, it's necessary to make up a compound noun, as clunky as that may be. In my novels: "non-being," "non-destiny," "non-love," "non-thought," "non-return."


**NON-BEING.** "Like non-being, death—tender and bluish." We can't say, "Like the void, death—tender and bluish," because the void isn't bluish. Which is proof that non-being and the void are two totally different things.


**NON-THOUGHT.** We can't translate this by the "absence of thought." The absence of thought marks a non-reality, a flight from reality. It's impossible to say that an absence is aggressive or that it is growing. In contrast, non-thought marks a reality, a power; so I can say, "invasive non-thought";

"the non-thought of received ideas"; "mass media non-thought"; etc.

**NOVEL.** Prose's crowning glory where an author, through made-up subjectivities (characters), examines one of life's big themes, making sure to press all the way to the end.

**NOVEL (and me).** Of everything I've written, only the novels warrant an opus number. (*Laughable Loves* is an experimental novel.) And yet I'll add one play: *Jacques and His Master*—a dramatic homage to a novel. As for my essays, opus numbers go only for those on the art of the novel. (See: **OPUS**.)

**NOVEL (and poetry).** 1857: the most important year in the nineteenth century. Baudelaire's *Les Fleurs du mal*: the height of lyric poetry. *Madame Bovary*: for the first time, a novel took up the conditions of poetry (the intention of "searching everywhere for beauty"; the importance of each specific word; the intense melody of the text; the demand for originality applied to each and every detail). In 1857, lyric poetry passed the baton to the novel's poetry. The history of the novel moving forward would be that of the "novel as a form of poetry." But to *take up the conditions of poetry* is something entirely different from a *lyrical* turn in the novel (to renounce its capacity for irony, to turn away from the exterior world, to transform the novel into a personal confession, to decorate it with ornamentation). The most important poetic novelists are *antilyric*: Flaubert, Joyce, Kafka, Gombrowicz. A novel = antilyric poetry.

★ NOVEL (European). The *European* novel developed in Central Europe in the first years of modernity, and it represents a historical entity in and of itself that, much later, would extend beyond the geography of Europe per se (into North and South America, in particular). By the richness of its forms, by the blinding intensity of its evolution, by its social position, the European novel (just like European music) is without compare.

NOVELIST (and writer). I'm rereading Sartre's essay "Why Write?" Not even once does he use the words "novel" or "novelist." He only talks about the "prose writer." It's a meaningful distinction. The writer has original ideas and an inimitable voice. He can use whatever form (including the novel), and everything he writes, being identifiable by his thinking and his voice, belongs in his oeuvre.

The novelist doesn't make much of his own ideas. He's an explorer who, while searching here and there, manages to uncover an unknown aspect of existence, which only a novel can clarify and make visible. He isn't caught up in his voice but by a form, and he chases after it. Only the forms that respond to the needs of his dream make up his oeuvre.

The writer delves into the spiritual map of his time, nation, and eventually the history of ideas.

The only context where the value of a novel is made clear is in the history of the European novel. The novelist owes nothing to anyone, except Cervantes.

★ **NOVELIST** (and the novelist's life). "The artist must make posterity think that he never existed," Flaubert said. Maupassant prevented his portrait from appearing in a series of famous writers. "The private life of a man and his face don't belong to the public," he said. Hermann Broch said the following about himself, Musil, and Kafka: "Not one of us has a real biography." This doesn't mean that their lives lacked interesting events, but that their lives weren't destined to be distinguished, to be public, to become life-writing. When Karel Čapek is asked why he doesn't write poetry, he says, "Because I hate talking about myself." The distinctive characteristic of a novelist is they don't want to talk about themselves. "I hate sticking my nose into the intimate details of the lives of great writers, and no biography can ever remove the veil from my life," Nabokov said. Italo Calvino warned others: he was resolved to never say a single true word to others about his life. And Faulkner wanted "to be a nobody, kept out of history, leaving no trace at all, other than what is in my books." (Let's emphasize "books" and "published," and not manuscripts, letters, and journals.) According to a famous metaphor, the novelist destroys the house of his life in order to build another with its bricks: the house of novels. With this in mind, the biographies of a novelist undo what the novelist did, and redo what he had undone. Biographies, which add nothing to art, cannot bring light, value, or meaning to a novel. When Kafka attracts more attention than Joseph K., then his posthumous death is underway.


**OBSCENITY.** In a foreign language, we use words that are obscene, but we don't really have the feel for them. An obscenity, pronounced with an accent, becomes humorous. The difficulty of being obscene with a foreign woman. Obscenity: the deepest root of national pride.


**OCTAVIO.** I was in the middle of constructing this little dictionary when the horrible earthquake struck Mexico, where Octavio Paz and his wife, Marie-Jo, live. On September 27, I turned over the final version to Pierre Nora, and that night there was a telephone call from Octavio. I opened a bottle to celebrate his good health. And I made his first name, so dear to me, really so dear, the 55th of these 89 words.

**OEUVRE.** "From the first draft to the finished work, the artist proceeds in a crawl." I'll never forget this line by Holan. And I refuse to put *Letters to Felice* on the same level as *The Castle*.

**OLD AGE.** "The old scholar watched the raucous young people, and he suddenly understood that he was the only one in the hall who possessed the privilege of freedom, because he was old; it's only when you're old that a person can ignore the opinion of the herd, the opinion of the public, and of the future. The old person is focused on death's arrival, and death doesn't have eyes or ears, the old person doesn't need to please anyone; the old person can do and say whatever they want to do and say" (*Life Is Elsewhere*). Rembrandt and Picasso. Bruckner and Janáček.

**OPUS.** The wonderful habit of composers. They give an opus number only to their works they consider to be "first-rate." They don't give an opus number to their juvenilia, to something written on a whim, or from an exercise. Take Beethoven's *Ten Variations on a Theme by Salieri*, which doesn't have an opus number, it's really a weak piece, but that shouldn't upset us because the composer himself warned us. A fundamental question for every artist: What work is their first "great" one? Janáček didn't find his originality until he was forty-five years old. It's painful for me to listen to the few works that remain from his earlier period. Before his death, Debussy destroyed all his sketches, everything he'd left incomplete. It's the least that an author can do for his good work: sweep away the chaff.


**ORDINARINESS.** Not banality, not vulgarity. The quality of someone who doesn't try to stick out, who is innocently and unaggressively ordinary. The magic spell, the sweetness of the ordinary: Lucie in *The Joke*.


**ORGASM.** The manuscript of an American translation of my work: Wherever I had pleasure, voluptuousness, or jouissance, the translator put "orgasm." One character (who was an epic lover) had hair that smelled of women. Translator: His hair smelled like a woman's orgasm. Orgasmocentrism.

**ORGASMOCENTRISM.** "It wasn't easy to give her [an orgasm], either. 'Faster,' she'd urge him on, 'faster,' then 'Take it easy, take it easy,' and then again 'Harder, harder.' She was like a coxswain shouting orders to the crew of a racing shell. Completely caught up in her own erogenous zones, she would guide his hand to the right place at the right time. Whenever he looked at her, he would see her impatient eyes and the feverish thrashings of her body—a portable apparatus for manufacturing the minor explosion that had become the meaning, the goal of her life."

**PARADISE.** "In Paradise . . . people weren't yet destined to be people. . . . Nostalgia for Paradise is the desire we have to not be people" (*The Unbearable Lightness of Being*).

**PASS AWAY** (to bury). The beauty of a word doesn't rest in the phonetic harmony of its syllables, but in the semantic associations that its sonority evokes. When a piano key is depressed, it sets off harmonic vibrations that the listener isn't aware of but that resonate nevertheless, and so each word is surrounded by a procession of other words that resonate with it, at the edge of perception.

One example: It has always seemed to me that the verb "to pass away" expunges, mercifully, the "terrifyingly material" side of the grimmest subject matter. It's as if the sonority of the phrase takes you to a place where you don't think about where you're going. To pass away where? Gauze curtains and velvet armchairs. (But this is a foreigner's perception. I could easily be wrong.) (See: **CACHE, FORSAKEN, LAZINESS, SEMPITERNAL.**)


**PHILOSOPHY.** Philosophical passages: the most difficult to translate. Their specificity as well as their beauty must be exact (each semantic misstep betrays the thought in question). The beauty of thinking is evident in the *poetic forms of thought.* I know three: (1) aphorism; (2) litany; and (3) metaphor. (See: **APHORISM, LITANY, METAPHOR.**)


**POLITICS.** We don't pronounce this word in the same way as others do. In the mouths of politicians and journalists, the first syllable explodes like a bullet shot from a gun: "It's a *p*olitical problem!" The more powerless politics are to meet the world's major challenges (debilitating overpopulation, the out-of-control growth of technology, the devastation of the earth, the death of culture), the more the first syllable "po-" gets drunk on its own power.

**PSEUDONYM.** I dream of a world where writers would be required by law to keep their identities secret and to use pseudonyms. The advantages: the strict curtailing of graphomania; the reduction of aggressiveness in the literary world.

**REPETITION.** There are translators who want to ameliorate the style of their authors and so replace repetitions of the same word with synonyms. "Repeating yourself like this isn't possible in French," they say. And yet one of the most beautiful prose passages in the French language starts like this: "I was desperately in love with the Comtesse de . . . ; I was twenty years old and I was naïve. She deceived me, I got angry, she left me. I was naïve, I missed her. I was twenty years old, because I was naïve—still deceived, but no longer abandoned—I thought myself to be the best-loved lover, and therefore the happiest of men."[*] Just try to replace

---

[*] Vivant Denon, *No Tomorrow*, trans. Lydia Davis (New York Review Books, 2009), 5.

these repetitions with synonyms: the charm of the text will disappear.


REWRITING. Interviews, literary conversations, talks. Adaptations, transcriptions, books made into movies, into TV shows. Rewriting in the guise of the spirit of the age where journalism is king and where the precision of the thought and the image is an anachronistic luxury. "It makes me think that one day all past culture will be completely rewritten and completely forgotten behind the rewrite" (introduction to *Jacques and His Master*). And "Death to all those who allow themselves to rewrite what was already written! Impale them and burn them over a low flame! Castrate them and cut off their ears!" (the Master in *Jacques and His Master*).


★ RHYTHM. I'm horrified whenever I hear my heartbeat because it reminds me that my life is finite. This is why I've always imagined something macabre when I look at the bar lines on a musical score. But the most skilled masters of rhythm knew how to silence this monotonous and predictable regularity. The masters of polyphony: counterpoint with its horizontal movement weakens the importance given to the measure. Beethoven: In his last period, it's almost impossible to make out the time signature, especially in slow movements, where the rhythm is so complicated. This is the reason for my admiration of Olivier Messiaen: On the back of his technique of additive rhythm, he invented an unforeseeable and incalculable temporal structure. Received thinking: The genius of rhythm is manifested through ostentatious regularity. Wrong. The oppressive rhythmic primitiveness of rock: The beating of the heart is amplified so that we don't forget for a single second our march toward death's door.

**SEMPITERNAL.** Only French has a word that is so untethered to the idea of eternity. Oral associations: to feel pity for someone—clown—pitiful—dull—eternal; the pitiful clown on this dull eternal earth.

**SLAV.** Six years ago, a friend showed me her copy of *The Joke*. In pencil, she'd underlined the sentence: "Behind the ship of our quarrel, I saw the healing waters of time converge. . . ." She had written in the margin: "The Slavic imagination." She didn't know that "the ship of our quarrel" was one of the translator's many additions. As for the word "Slav," she had understood it just as I do. Deregulated rendering of the world in poetry, showy emotions, simulated depths, long glances that seem to mean something yet accuse you of not getting the gist . . . this is my idea of the Slavic soul. The Slavic soul, a purely negative construct.


**SMILE.** Immobile and stuck on the face; a sign of extraordinary wickedness.


**SOVIET.** I don't use this adjective. The Union of Soviet Socialist Republics: "Four words, four lies" (Cornelius Castoriadis). The Soviet people: a lexical screen behind which the long Russification of the empire is asked to be forgotten. The term "Soviet" applies not only to the aggressive nationalism of Communist Russia but also to the national nostalgia of dissidents. It lets them believe, as though in an act of magic, that Russia (the real Russia) is something other than the Soviet state and that it will live on in its pure essence despite any and all accusations. The German consciousness; traumatized, made to feel guilty after the Nazis; Thomas Mann: the cruel questioning of the German spirit. The maturity of Polish culture: Gombrowicz who so happily violates "Polishness." It's unthinkable for the Russians to criticize "Russianness," an immaculate essence. There's no Mann or Gombrowicz among them.

**TASTE** (good taste). *The Farewell Waltz*: "The sadness that wafted from Klima's last sentences had, for her, an agreeable odor. She breathed it in, like it was roast pork." The German translator changed it so his sadness "made her feel good, like a bubble bath." Comparing sadness to roast pork seemed vulgar to him! It was no one other than the Wotan of Good Taste in flesh and blood who had censured me!

**TENDER.** "The man crossed the room holding Jaromil firmly in the air, while he floundered like a tender and hopeless fish" (*Life Is Elsewhere*).

★ **TESTAMENT.** Nowhere and in no other published or reproduced form will any of my works appear except those books published by Gallimard Publishers, as per their most recent catalog. No annotated editions are approved of. And no adaptations. (See: **OEUVRE, OPUS, REWRITING.**) [*Statement issued on the republication of* The Art of the Novel *in 1995.*]

**TRANSLATORS.** I often criticize translators, and it's unfair. They are poorly paid, underappreciated, and generally mistreated; and we want them to do diametrically opposite things: to be at the author's level—while at the same time to be entirely subordinated to the author. Terrible. And still they are the ones who are allowed to live in the supranational space of world literature, and they are the humble builders of Europe and the West.

★ TRANSPARENCY. In politics and journalism, this word means: making public people's private lives. This brings us back to André Breton and his desire to live in a *glass house* where everyone can see in. A glass house: an old utopia and at the same time one of the most frightening aspects of modern times. Rule of thumb: the more opaque the affairs of state become, the most transparent the affairs of the private individual must grow; while the bureaucracy represents a *public entity* and so is anonymous, secret, coded, unintelligible; the *private individual* is obliged to reveal his health, his finances, his family situation and, if it were for the mass media to decide, he would no longer find a single private moment for love, sickness, and death. The desire to violate the intimacy of other people is an immemorial form of aggressiveness that, today, is institutionalized (the bureaucracy with its files, the press with its reporters), morally justified (the right to information has become the first human right), and made poetic (by the beautiful word: transparency).

**UGLY.** After suffering so much from the cops and her husband's affairs, Tereza says: "Prague has become ugly." Translators want to use words like "horrible" and "unbearable" instead of "ugly." They find it illogical to react to a *moral* situation with an *aesthetic* judgment. But the word "ugly" is perfect: When twenty-seven Bohemian aristocrats were decapitated in the Old Town Square in 1621, Prague was struck dumb, but its beauty wasn't sullied. Yet the ugliness of the modern world is omnipresent and oppressive, and it makes itself known whenever we run into the slightest trouble.

**UNIFORM.** "Since reality consists in the uniformity of calculable reckoning, man, too, must enter monotonous uniformity in order to keep up with what is real. A man without uni-form today already gives the impression of being something unreal which no longer belongs."* The road-weary K. isn't looking for fraternity (as the sentimental "humanist" reading would have it) but is hopelessly looking for a uni-form. Without this uniform, without the uniform of an employee, he hasn't "kept up" with "the real." He gives "the impression of being something unreal." Kafka was the first (before Heidegger) to seize on this fundamental change in situation: Yesterday, we could still see an ideal, a chance, a victory in the plurality of forms,

---

* Martin Heidegger, *The End of Philosophy*, trans. Joan Stambaugh (Harper & Row, 1973), 108

in the escape from the uniform; tomorrow, the loss of the uniform will represent an absolute penalty, a rejection beyond the bounds of the human. Since Kafka's time, thanks to the superstructures that calculate and plan life, the uniformization of the world has greatly advanced. But when a phenomenon becomes general, quotidian, and omnipresent, we no longer see it. In the euphoria of a uni-form life, people no longer see the uniform they wear.

**VALUE.** The structuralism of the 1960s threw value into question. And the founder of structuralist aesthetics said, "Only the hypothesis of an objective aesthetic value, constantly being perceived anew and realized anew in the most varied modifications, gives any meaning to the historical development of art."* Questioning aesthetic value is the same as trying to delimit and name the discovery, the innovations, and the new light that a work throws onto humanity. Only a work that has become valued (the work whose novelty has been identified and named) can become part of the "historical evolution of art," which isn't a simple series of facts but a pursuit of values. When we set aside the question of value, satisfying ourselves with a thematic, sociological, formalist description of a work (or of a historical period, culture, etc.),

---

* Jan Mukařovský, *Aesthetic Function, Norm and Value as Social Facts*, tr. Mark E. Suino, Michigan Slavic Contributions (Ann Arbor: University of Michigan Press, 1970), 94.

when we say that all cultures and all cultural activities are of equal worth (Bach and rock, comic strips and Proust), when art criticism (meditation on value) no longer finds the time of day to say anything, then "the historical evolution of art" will lose meaning, it will perish, becoming an immense and absurd warehouse of all that was ever written, painted, made.

**VULGARITY.** In 1965, I showed the manuscript of *The Joke* to a friend, who happened to be an excellent Czech philosopher. He scolded me roundly for being vulgar and for undercutting the human dignity of Helena. But how is one to avoid being vulgar, which is so necessary in life? The domain of vulgarity is found below, where the body and its needs reign. Vulgarity: the humiliating submission of the soul to the reign of the nether world. Joyce's *Ulysses* was the first novel to capture the immense importance of the theme of vulgarity.

**YOUTH.** "A wave of self-hatred overwhelmed me, anger against my youth, against the stupid *age of the lyric*. . . ." (*The Joke*).

# PRAGUE,
## A Disappearing Poem

# 1

Prague: this dramatic and aching center of Western destiny that slowly slips further into the mists of Eastern Europe, where it never belonged. Prague: the first city east of the Rhine with a university. Prague: the scene, in the fifteenth century, of the first large European revolution, the cradle of the Reformation. Prague: the city that stoked the Thirty Years' War, the capital of the Baroque and its follies. Prague: which in 1968 vainly tried to westernize the socialism imported from the cold East.

Atlantis comes to mind. And it's not simply the relatively recent political annexation that has made this city seem so far away and so hard to understand. The Czech language, forbidding to foreigners, has always been a barrier, like an opaque mirror, between Prague and the other Europe.

Outside of Bohemia, what people know about my country has always come through secondhand materials. Its history was written according to German sources. People have opined about the work of Antonin Dvořák and Leoš Janáček, and yet their letters, their theoretic works, their milieu remain unknown and unknowable. Still today, people examine Prague's role in Kafka's work despite their complete ignorance about Czech culture. The Prague Spring fosters brilliant speculation, while the newspapers and the literary journals of the time remain untouched. Structuralism's massive impact on the entire world originated in Prague, but the work of its founder, the Prague native Jan Mukařovský, remains unknown, because he wrote in Czech.

It often seems to me that hidden within European culture there is another European culture, that of the small nations with their weird languages—the culture of the Polish, Czechs, Catalans, and Danish. It's assumed that these small nations imitate the large ones. But it's an illusion. They're very different.

The perspective of a small country isn't the same as a large one. The Europe of the small nations is *another Europe*; it has another perspective, and its thinking often forms the true counterpoint of the Europe of large nations.

# 2

*It's noon I'm seated beneath a colorful parasol*
*In all its glory Prague lies at my feet*
*It looks like a magical city I once imagined*
*It looks like a dream built by fantastical workers*
*It looks like a throne like the city where magic was born*

## Prague, A Disappearing Poem

*It looks like a volcanic citadel carved in stone by a feverish madman*
—VITĚZSLAV NEZVAL, "PRAGUE IN THE RAIN"

Some cultural eras of Europe have been marked by the spirit of rationalism and others have been inspired by the irrational, and yet we can say that the second type has dominated the history of Prague: the Gothic, the mannerist ways of the late Renaissance, and especially the Baroque.

At the end of the Renaissance, the court of Emperor Rudolf II was the European center for esoteric sciences and fantastical arts. It was in those years that Prague knew Kepler, the astronomer and astrologer, and Arcimboldi, the Salvador Dalí of the sixteenth century, and Löw, the important humanist Jewish rabbi who according to legend created the first artificial person, a robot, the Golem.

The Thirty Years' War, which interrupted Rudolf's reign, was a catastrophe in which the Czech people were almost wiped out under the pressure of forced re-Catholicization and Germanization. It was under the hypnosis of Baroque art that this massive brainwashing was effectuated, with the goal of transforming a Protestant Slav nation into a Catholic German one. All of its expressive, dramatic statues, all of its fascinating, exuberant churches are "flowers of evil," the fruit of oppression. (The complicity of beauty and evil is a very Prague experience, and we are all initiated into it from our childhoods.)

The Baroque era led not only to the spread of architectural and musical beauty but also to the stifling of freethinking, literature, the novel, and philosophy, which for two centuries (the sixteenth and seventeenth) were almost nonexistent. The absence of rationalism and realism was compensated by the hypertrophy of the irrational and the fantastical: legends, fairy tales, exaltation, a morbid imagination. It was then that the extraordinary disequilibrium of this city and this country was born in its literatures (Czech as well as German). Moving forward, the magical was always for Prague much more important than the real. To wit, André Breton, referring to Nezval's poetry, called Prague the "European capital of magic."

In the streets of Prague, Franz Kafka could have met one but only one important German writer of the previous generation: Gustav Meyrink, the author of fantastical stories. In 1902, Meyrink published his first story, "The Burning Soldier," in *Simplicissimus*. The story is about a soldier who suddenly comes down with a horrible fever that keeps rising, first to 70 degrees Celsius, then to 80 degrees, and, as a result, everything around him goes up in flames, and everyone flees. This is the story of the inexplicable and unjustifiable metamorphosis of a man into a monster. Ten years later,

Kafka wrote his first famous short story: the story of Gregor Samsa, who is transformed into a cockroach in a similarly inexplicable and unjustifiable way.

Kafka's work both preserves and exceeds Prague's heritage of magic: His major innovation is not in having brought a fantastical imagination to the novel. In other words, he was entirely in keeping with the tradition of the capital of magic. How he radically exceeded this tradition (which separates *Metamorphosis* from the work of Meyrink) was in adding the real to the fantastical (the real of detailed observations with a social outlook) so that his dreamlike imagination isn't, like in Romanticism, a dreamy evasion or pure subjectivity but a way of penetrating real life, to unmask it, and to catch it off guard.

He was the first to effectuate the alchemical fusion of dreams and reality (before the surrealists got to it), the first to create an autonomous universe where the real appears fantastical and where the fantastical unmasks the real. Modern art owes the discovery of this alchemy to Kafka's Prague heritage.

# 3

Jaroslav Hašek was born the same year as Kafka and died one year earlier. Both remained in their native city all their lives and, according to legend, they knew each other, as they participated in the same meetings of Czech anarchists.

It would be difficult to find two writers more different in their basic natures. Kafka, a vegetarian. Hašek, a drunk. The one, cautious; the other, eccentric. One wrote books considered difficult, coded, hermetic; the other wrote extremely popular books excluded from so-called serious literature.

And yet both artists, outwardly so different, were born from the same society, in the same time and milieu, and they spoke of the same thing: the solitary person confronted with a society that has been transformed into a gigantic bureaucratic apparatus (Kafka) or a military one (Hašek): K. at trial or standing before the castle; Švejk facing the totalitarianism of the Austro-Hungarian army.

Just a little while later, in 1920, another Prague writer, Karel Čapek, wrote a play entitled *R.U.R.* about robots. (The neologism "robot" originated here before spreading across the globe.) Robots, built by men, start to rebel. Endowed with strict discipline and a lack of feeling, they end up wiping humans off the face of the earth and installing their own empire. This scenario of the disappearance of the human under a fantastical totalitarian wave became, for Čapek, an abiding obsession, a lasting nightmare, across all of his work.

Just after World War I, when European literature tended to fall into the seductive embrace of a radiant vision of the future and a revolutionary eschatology, these Prague writers were the first to look behind progress to see its dark, menacing, morbid side.

Since these are the most representative writers of their country, we can see in them not random chance but a specific way of looking at the world that was common to them—yes, this disabused way of looking characteristic of the *other Europe* of small nations and minorities, which were the objects and not the subjects of events: the Jewish minority, encircled by so many nations, where they led their lives of silent anguish (Kafka); the Czech minority, folded into the Austrian Empire, whose politics and wars didn't concern them at all (Hašek); the newly born Czech state, a minority itself, in the center of the Europe of large nations, which headed directly toward the next catastrophe without ever asking the Czechs what they wanted (Čapek).

Writing an important *humorous* novel on the subject of *war*, which Hašek did in *The Good Soldier Švejk*, would have caused a scandal in France or Russia. It presupposes a particular idea of the comic (which never steps aside, which undercuts the serious everywhere it goes) and a particular worldview. Neither Jews nor Czechs identify strongly with History, that's to say, with the serious, and with the meaningfulness of events. Their immemorial experience has taught them not to venerate this Goddess and to praise her wisdom. So, the Europe of small nations, better protected against the demagoguery of hope, has held a more lucid notion of the future than the Europe of large nations, which are always ready to sup from the goblet of their glorious historical mission.

# 4

What makes Kafka's and Hašek's books immortal isn't their descriptions of the totalitarian machine per se but the presence of the two great Josephs, Joseph K. and Joseph Švejk, who personify our basic choices in the face of this machine.

What is Joseph K.'s attitude? He wants to understand the inner workings of the trial, which is as opaque as the will of Calvin's God; he wants to understand the trial, and he wants to make himself understood. So he becomes a *zealous defendant*: he rushes to the courthouse to be on time even though no one has told him when his case might be heard. When the two executioners lead him to his fated end, he protects them from the glances of the city cops. The trial is no longer the enemy; it's an inaccessible truth that he wishes to know. He wants to force the mad world to make sense, and his effort costs him his life.

And what is Švejk's attitude? At the beginning of World War I, which began with the invasion of Serbia, Joseph

## Prague, A Disappearing Poem

Švejk, though in excellent health, connives to have himself pushed through the streets of Prague in a wheelchair, all the way to the army recruitment office, where he raises his two borrowed crutches and shouts with outsized enthusiasm: "Onward to Serbia! Belgrade here I come!" All the residents of Prague who see him get a good chuckle out of it, but the authorities can do nothing to stop him. He learns how to mime perfectly the gestures of the world that he finds himself in, he repeats the slogans, he participates in the ceremonies. But because he doesn't take them seriously at all, he transforms them into an enormous joke.

During a military mass, attended in part by enemy soldiers held as prisoners in the garrison, the chaplain Katz, drunk as always, rolls into a long sermon forgiving these soldiers their sins. Švejk, wearing baggy prisoner shorts, begins to weep noisily. In order to make his friends laugh, he pretends to be moved by the chaplain's words. This comic sense saves Švejk's internal integrity, even in the conditions of total manipulation inflicted on soldiers during war. Švejk has succeeded in living and surviving in a mad world because, in contrast to the other Joseph, he refuses to acknowledge the meaning of that world.

It's fascinating to see the continuity linking Prague's fiction and its reality: Švejk and K., these important figures of the imagination, dissolve back into life itself. It's true that Kafka's novels have been taken off the shelves of public libraries, but everywhere in Prague today you can see their scenes being enacted. That's why they have achieved universal status and are cited in everyday conversations in Prague, no less so than Hašek's literature, which was intended to be popular.

During and after the famous 1951 Slánský trial, we saw thousands of Joseph Ks. There were innumerable copycat trials at every level of society: condemnations, firings, censures, persecutions, and all with the constant self-criticism of guilt-ridden victims who at all costs wanted to understand the trial and make themselves understood by it, who strived up to the last minute to find something intelligible in the movements of the mad machine that was crushing them underfoot. *Zealous defendants*, they wanted to help their executioners and, even at the stake, they would shout: "Long live the Party!" (They saw a moral grandeur in this grotesque devotion; the poet Laco Novomeský, after his release from prison, wrote a series of poems on the glory of his faithfulness. Prague residents have nicknamed these poems "The Gratitude of Joseph K.")

Švejk's ghost is no less present in the streets of Prague. Early on after the Russian invasion of 1968, I attended a large student meeting. Everyone was waiting for Gustáv Husák, the new Party leader, put in place by the Russians, who was going to give a speech. But he hadn't even had the chance to open his mouth when everyone launched into a chant, "Long live Husák! Long live the Party!" It lasted for five minutes, then fifteen minutes, and Husák, blushing more and more violently, was forced to leave. Without a doubt, it was Švejk's genius that had led the students to unleash this unforgettable deluge of applause.

In these two examples of "Long live the Party!" (the condemned at the stake and the students in front of Husák), I see two extreme attitudes in regard to totalitarian power. Yet they had already existed in Prague's literature for thirty years.

# 5

"Enough psychology!" Kafka wrote in his diary, and Hašek could very well have written the same line. Who really is this Švejk, always acting a fool, incessantly speaking in contradictions? What does he really think? What does he feel? What are the motivations for his inexplicable behavior? That this novel is a popular and apparently easy read shouldn't trick us into misrecognizing the truly unconventional way that Švejk is constructed as a character.

This antipsychological attitude of Prague's authors predates the celebrated example of American novelists who sheared introspective passages from their tradition in favor of action and plot, trying to capture the world through exteriority, through its visual and tangible aspects. The gist of the Prague writer's quest is a little different: It's not about love for virile action or description of exteriority; it's about another way of understanding people.

This new way of looking at the human condition is reflected in a shocking circumstance: *The two Josephs have no past.* What about their families? What happened to them as children?

Did their mother and father love them? How did they get to where they are? We don't know anything about any of this, and it's in this nothingness that we find a rupture. Because what used to excite novelists above all else, and even today, is the act of delving into psychological motivations, that's to say, the reconstruction of a mysterious link between past and present action, the pursuit of "lost time," where you can find the brilliant infinity of the soul.

Kafka doesn't renounce introspection; but as we try to follow his logic from one chapter to the next, it's not the richness of his soul that bowls us over. K.'s reasoning is strictly limited by the situation, both autocratic and despotic, that completely absorbs him. Prague authors don't write about the nature of the treasure hidden in the human psyche but about human possibility in the trap that the world has become. The projector is stuck on a single situation and on the person who confronts this situation. It's in this singular attitude that we find the "infinity" that must be explored to its farthest reaches.

So, at the same time that Marcel Proust and James Joyce achieved the limits of the possible through their introspective virtuosity, Kafka's "Enough psychology!" (realized in equal measure by Hašek) lays bare another novelistic aesthetic. Twenty, thirty years later, Sartre would speak of focusing not on *characters* but on *situations*, "all the basic situations of human life," whose metaphysics he would attempt to capture. In this aesthetic climate, after World War II, the tendency of Prague novelists became more well known. But it's in their work that we can appreciate the basic sense of this change in orientation: *Interior* motivations don't mean much in the world where *exterior* factors limit people in an ever greater degree.

The new novelistic orientation that rejects the conventions of the psychological novel is historically linked, then, to the foreboding of a totalitarian world. It's a coincidence rife with meaning.

# 6

In his well-known biography of Kafka, Klaus Wagenbach writes at length of Prague and its culture, and yet he doesn't know Czech and so doesn't know what he's talking about.

It's easy to understand why he sees Prague as nothing but a provincial town, cut off from the world, a little down-at-heel, where the work of the great shut-in fell from the sky like a stray meteorite.

But Prague was anything but provincial. First, the city was the capital of the Czech people who, full of vitality and ambition, had already begun their national renaissance. Then, in the face of unilateral German influence, the international orientation of the Czech was very cosmopolitan: They were pro-French, pro-English, pro-Russian. But especially (in the arts) pro-French. Finally, it was due to how Czech culture, which was dynamic and modernist, was living hand in hand with a minority German culture in a competitive and fruitful way.

Yes, there was the Prague of the Czech majority (45,000 people at the beginning of the century), and the Prague of the German minority (33,000 people, mostly bourgeois and intellectuals). But there was also the *integrated* Prague of Kafka, who was bilingual. And not just him, but all his friends, the Jewish writers Max Brod, Franz Werfel, Egon Erwin Kisch, Oskar Baum, who, setting aside national quarrels between the Czechs and the Germans, knew how to draw on and integrate the traditions of the two peoples.

In his diary from 1911, Kafka describes his meeting with the painter Willi Nowak, who had just finished a series of portraits of Max Brod, using a technique familiar from

Picasso: The first portrait was faithful, while those that followed relied less and less on the model, to culminate in abstraction. This was Kafka's first (but not last) encounter with Cubist painting. His diary reveals his interest in it and his understanding of its techniques, which contrasts drolly with Brod's confusion, recounted by Kafka in a tone of amical irony.

While we're given to speculate endlessly about Kafka's ties to Czech anarchists (ties that have never been definitively proven), we forget the much more important and historical contacts that he had with Czech modern art.

From the beginning of the century, the Czech side of Prague participated passionately in the adventure of modern art. It was in these years that Prague and Paris developed their strong bond: Alfons Mucha and František Kupka made their mark on French art and, in the years before the war, Parisian Cubism found nowhere else than in Prague such a rich and original response.

Max Brod coined the term "der Prager Kreis," or the Prague Circle, for the group of Jewish writers who gathered around him and Kafka. From 1925, we can speak of another Prague Circle, namely, those linguists and aestheticians (Vilém Mathesius, Jan Mukařovský, Roman Jakobson, etc.) who created the word "structuralism" and who proclaimed themselves "structuralists." Before the eruption of war, Jakobson left Prague for the United States, and structuralism became a dominant current of thinking during the next several decades.

This wasn't a coincidence: Prague was one of the most dynamic centers of modern thought and sensibility.

# 7

There were several reasons why Prague was predestined to become the cradle and first center of structuralism: the moral prestige of the young republic and of President Masaryk, a champion of democracy admired across Europe, and an author of an important philosophical oeuvre that influenced structural linguistics; the welcoming, cosmopolitan climate, sensitive to foreign tastes, which connected Czech, German, Russian, and Polish linguists around a single research subject; the autochthonous aesthetic tradition of Czech formalism (the "Prague School of Aesthetics," at the end of the nineteenth century) and the intensity of linguistic research (concentrated before the war around Vilém Mathesius, a student of Masaryk); and finally (and especially) the dynamic Czech avant-garde, which found its best friends and allies in the structuralists.

The work of the Czech structuralists was characterized by a taste for concrete analysis, its wide scope (from modern poetry to medieval texts, from Čapek's prose to folklorist and ethnographic studies), its love for clarity, and its ambition to focus exclusively on essential matters. The crutches of preciousness and dogmatism that would later shroud structuralism with ridicule were unknown to them.

The alliance between structuralist theory and postwar modernism was an entirely unique phenomenon. The aesthetic theories that accompanied modernist movements tended to be apologetic. This wasn't the case with structuralism in Prague: It was linked to the avant-garde but for a much more general reason: *to understand and to defend art in its specificity.*

If a novel (a poem, a film) is content put into a form, then it would follow that it's only an ideological message in disguise: Its aesthetic character collapses. The ideological reading of a novel (and this is what is asked of us always and without letup) is as reductive, mind-numbing, and flattening as any ideological reduction of reality itself. If we insist on the specificity of art, it's not to evade the real; much to the contrary, it's the desire to see a tree in a tree, a painting in a painting. It's resisting against the *reductive forces* that destroy both people and art.

In their understanding that a work of art is an organism where everything is at once form and content and where everything is irreducible to another language (like that of ideological explication), the Prague structuralists took up the defense of the irreducibility of human experience itself.

It was as though they shared with Kafka, Čapek, and others their anguish (which is so Prague) in the face of the *reductive forces* that were drawing nearer from the depths of the future with such implacable weight.

# 8

French surrealism is often thought of as a revolt against Western rationalism, against Cartesian coldness. Yet, curiously, this revolt against rationalism quickly transformed into the rationalism of theory-driven manifestos that left traces in French national memory (irony of ironies) that were more lasting than surrealist art's fascinating lack of rationalism.

Czech surrealism had no cause to revolt against Czech Cartesianism, which never existed; rather, it represented an organic fulfillment of Prague's artistic tradition, the confirmation of its fascinating and irrational specificity.

Thanks to its natural roots in the cultural history of the country, what we call Czech surrealism (and what was no more than a prolongation of the autochthonous avant-garde currents, namely, that of "pietism") had, in terms of national literatures, an influence that greatly outweighed that of French surrealism in its own society. Almost all the leading personalities of modern Czech culture were marked by surrealism, magical thinking, and the imagination. To a surprising degree, the Czech public is exceptionally sensitive to this sort of beauty.

When I was a ten-year-old boy, I heard for the first time the poetry of Vitězslav Nezval, the most important Czech surrealist, when I was spending the summer in a Moravian village. In those days, students would return to their fathers' villages for summer vacation and would recite his poetry like it was magic. During evening walks through the wheat fields, they taught me all the poems of *Woman in the Plural*.

Due to the absence of an aristocracy and an entrenched bourgeoisie in Czech society, the Prague avant-garde was more closely aligned with ordinary people, labor, and nature. This interdependence became a part of its imagination. In my mind, I see the man Nezval, with his red and always excitable face; I hear him repeat the word "concrete," this adjective that represented for him the important quality of the modern imagination, which he wanted to be chock-full of perception, lived experiences, and memories.

"Instead of the lily as symbol of chastity, I prefer the one that I crushed one day when playing hide-and-seek as a child," he once said. Another time he said, "It's surprising to meet a distinguished sort of gentleman unable to understand modern poetry because he's looking obsessively for an allegorical meaning." He hated "art ideologues," who always ended up reducing poetry or a painting to a platitude, which only strips it of its essence. In the 1930s, with other Czech surrealists, he discovered and promoted Kafka, and he made fun of those who saw in the castle either grace, hell, or God but never the concrete absurdity of our times.

Understanding the imagination's magic not as a pale copy of life but as the "drunkenness of the concrete" seems to me, in short, the profound inclination of Czech modernism. This disposition tied Nezval, a surrealist, to his opposite, Vladimír Holan, whose poetry is sometimes compared to Rilke's or Valéry's. And yet, full of peasants, maids, drunks, and criminals, it cracks underneath the "weight of the concrete," and so is radically different from Rilke's or Valéry's.

## 9

What body of work could better shed light on the original character of Czech modernism than that of the composer Leoš Janáček? Along with Kafka, he was the most important figure of modern art in his country. Max Brod knew this better than others: Not only did Brod save and then relaunch Kafka's work in public but, less well known, he fought with the same passion for Janáček. He wrote marvelous analyses of his compositions, he translated his operas into German, and he published his first biography in 1924. His fight on behalf of this out-of-fashion and brilliant composer was so passionate and so important that Kafka didn't hesitate to compare it to the battle waged by French intellectuals on behalf of Dreyfus.

What's stunning in his music (and what is its largest shortcoming) is how it's entirely unclassifiable. In Mahler's last symphonies and in the first works of Schoenberg, musical Romanticism reached the end of the line. The young generation buried it in noise; the new composers buried an entire era that thought of music as mirror to the soul, confession, and expression. At this crucial juncture, Janáček found a new way forward in contemporary music. No one saw it but him. He followed this course by himself.

He too was opposed to Romantic music, but his polemic took a different tack. He critiqued Romanticism not for attempting to express the soul and its states, but for having failed in its attempt; for having cheated us; that instead of discovering naked sentiment, it had given us clichés, gestures, and poses. He wanted to unmask reality. That's why he didn't give up on the idea of music as expression but wanted, on the contrary, to eliminate every note that wouldn't be pure and naked expression. He arrived at a musical structure of unexpected expressivity and economy.

But isn't speaking of the truth of feelings the same as beating a dead horse? No. Before Messiaen, before Varèse, Janáček was possessed by nature, by birdsong. Most notably, he studied spoken language, its intonations, its melodies, its difficult rhythms. (In this field, he was the first and last.) He stole fragments of words from the streets, marketplaces, bustling train stations; and he stole them as a brazen photographer would (even the groans of his dying daughter didn't escape his attention), transcribing them as musical notations in his notebook. There are thousands of these notational fragments, kept today in a museum, which bear witness to the seriousness of his research: It was the quest for a form of musical semantics, as though he wanted to create a dictionary of feelings, or melodic formulae, to discover the mysterious link between music and psychology.

Whatever the objective value of these notebooks, his research represents the composer's orientation in a revealing way: He wanted to break from music as music (like a writer who tries not to write "literature"), and he wanted to find new sources of musical language closer to psychology and tied directly to life. He wanted to arrive at not only a new beauty (a new sonority, a new type of melody, a new construction) but also a greater *exactitude* (psychological exactitude) in the musical phrase, as he was persuaded that music was anthropological.

His efforts were neither utopian nor quixotic. He succeeded in creating a marvelous body of work in the last decades of his life, between the ages of fifty and seventy-four (he's assuredly the best "elderly" composer in the history of music):

incomparable choral works and a new aesthetic for opera that led to five masterpieces.

# 10

The year he died, Janáček wrote his last opera. It was his most beautiful yet, his best, truly his musical will and testament: *From the House of the Dead*, after Dostoevsky. How did he arrive at choosing this impossible subject, which must have disgusted the public—this prison reportage that told no story and that had no plot? What had inspired this sinister setting, which had nothing to do with the composer's own life?

It's true that its violently modern music changes the nineteenth-century penal colony into a concentration camp, and that this quintessentially contemporary spectacle stupefies us. But in 1928, in such pleasant times? What nightmare came to Janáček to inspire this dark vision?

It's impossible to explain. Nevertheless, my country has erected three central monuments of art in this century that represent three panels in the hellish triptych of the future: the bureaucratic labyrinth of Kafka, the military stupidity of Hašek, and the carceral despair of Janáček. Yes, between *The Trial* (1925) and *From the House of the Dead* (1930), everything was laid out for us in Prague, and History only had to arrive to mimic what fiction had already imagined.

The famous Prague coup d'état in 1948 brought about not only Kafkaesque trials, the stupidity forecast by Hašek, and prisons sprung from the imagination of Janáček but also the abolition of the culture that had anticipated them. We don't really have a handle on what then happened: After one thousand years of being a Western country, Czechoslovakia became part of the Eastern bloc. It became the place where the West (the colonizer par excellence) was then colonized, and where Western culture (which the world over views as possessive and aggressive) was destined to lose its identity. It is a historical injustice that this "counter-colonization" took place in a country that had never colonized anyone.

Then, right after the coup, the country organized large pogroms "against cosmopolitanism" (which was to say, against Western culture). To wit, the entire modern intellectual history of my country was blacklisted. This was when Mukařovský committed intellectual suicide and renounced his entire, important body of structuralist work. It was when Holan locked himself in an act of voluntary self-imprisonment in his Prague apartment, where he remains today.

Yet that wasn't the end. The cultural vitality of the country resisted and, little by little, it regained its foothold, thanks to stubbornness, collective will, and trickery: Everything that had been banned returned in the 1960s. It was nothing less than a war, the war of a culture fighting for its survival.

One of the largest battles was fought over Kafka. In 1963, Czech intellectuals organized an international conference in a Bohemian castle. Russian ideologues would never be able to forgive them this insolence. Official documents that justified the invasion of Czechoslovakia in 1968 referred to Kafka's rehabilitation as the first signal of the counter-revolution.

This argument would otherwise appear absurd; but it was less a sign of sheer stupidity than a foretaste of things to come. The invasion of Czechoslovakia wasn't only a victory for "dogmatic Communism" over "liberal Communism" (which is the popular explanation of the event) but also (an aspect that in hindsight would be the most important) the final annexation of a Western country by the civilization of Russian totalitarianism. I say *civilization* intentionally, and not the *political system*, or the *state*. It wasn't because he was anti-Communist or that he opposed the Soviet military that Kafka provoked Moscow's rage, but because he represented a culture foreign to the colonizer and so one that was not prone to being assimilated, even while Soviet culture was advancing politically across the world at the same time as it was regressing culturally toward its Byzantine past.

# 11

*Like a piece of paper in flames*
  *where the poem disappears . . .*
—VITĚZSLAV NEZVAL, WOMAN IN THE PLURAL

Prague's culture is as old as the West itself.

It was at its height between 1910 and 1940. After a bloody intermission, the 1960s rebounded like the last echo of its thousand-year-old history. Its culture woke up in a world where its own nightmares had become reality. Stuck in the totalitarian night, it was able to reflect upon these circumstances, judge them, ironize them, analyze them, and transform them into an object of its own intellectual experience. The genius of the small penetrated the arrogance of the large. Its humor corroded the horrors of ideological seriousness. Its concreteness stood against the largest *reductive forces* that History had ever unleashed. From this shock to its nervous system, an entire canon of works was born—theater, cinema, literature, philosophy, humor; an entire intellectual experience, which is unique and irreplaceable. As Holan said, "Only Christ would know how to paint / Pontius Pilate's wife."

At the time, the West didn't understand the meaning of this creative explosion, blinded as it was by its politicized vision of things (which was reductive). Rather, it only saw a confirmation of the vitality of socialism (the stupidity of the Left); and the West refused to see anything of value behind the facade of the Communist regime (the stupidity of the Right). A curtain of Western misinterpretations doubled the Soviet Union's Iron Curtain.

The Russian invasion of 1968 swept away the generation of the 1960s and, with it, the modern culture that had preceded it. Our books were imprisoned in the same cellars as Kafka's books and Czech surrealists. People were suffocating inside their lives; they were living side by side with the dead rendered doubly dead.

So that we fully understand the situation, we must realize that it's not only human rights, democracy, and justice that no longer exist in Prague, it's that an entire beautiful culture is today

*like a piece of paper in flames*
*where the poem disappears.*

# OTHER BOOKS BY MILAN KUNDERA

**FICTION**

*Ignorance*

Set in contemporary Prague, *Ignorance* takes up the complex and emotionally charged theme of exile and creates from it a literary masterpiece.

*Identity*

"A beguiling meditation on the illusions of self-image and desire."
—TIME OUT NEW YORK

"A fervent and compelling romance, a moving little fable about the anxieties of love and separateness."
—BALTIMORE SUN

*Slowness*

"Irresistible. . . . An ode to sensuous leisure."
—MIRABELLA

"Audacity, wit, and sheer brilliance."
—NEW YORK TIMES BOOK REVIEW

## Other Books by Milan Kundura

*Immortality*

From a woman's casual gesture to her swimming instructor springs a novel of the imagination that both embodies and articulates the great themes of existence.

> "Ingenious, witty, provocative, and formidably intelligent, both a pleasure and a challenge to the reader."
> —Washington Post Book World

*The Unbearable Lightness of Being*

> "Mr. Kundera's novel composed in the spirit of the late quartets of Beethoven is concerned with the opposing elements of freedom and necessity among a quartet of entangled lovers."
> —New Yorker

*The Book of Laughter and Forgetting*

> "*The Book of Laughter and Forgetting* calls itself a novel, although it is part fairy tale, part literary criticism, part political tract, part musicology, and part autobiography. It can call itself whatever it wants to, because the whole is genius."
> —New York Times

## Other Books by Milan Kundura

*Farewell Waltz*

*Farewell Waltz* poses the most serious questions with a blasphemous lightness that makes us see that the modern world has deprived us even of the right to tragedy.

> "*Farewell Waltz* shocks. Black humor. Farcical ferocity."
> —LE POINT (PARIS)

*Life Is Elsewhere*

> "A remarkable portrait of an artist as (Paris) a young man."
> —NEWSWEEK

> "A sly and merciless lampoon of revolutionary romanticism."
> —TIME

*Laughable Loves*

> "Kundera takes some of Freud's most cherished complexes and irreverently whirls them about in acts of legerdemain that capture our darkest, deepest human passions.... Complex, full of mockeries and paradoxes."
> —CLEVELAND PLAIN DEALER

# Other Books by Milan Kundura

## *The Joke*
A student's innocent joke incurs hard punishment in Stalinist Czechoslovakia.

> "A thoughtful, intricate, ambivalent novel."
> —John Updike

## *The Festival of Insignificance*
> "There is a timeless quality to his philosophy about the importance of laughter. . . . Kundera is still the powerful and incisive writer he always was."
> —New York Times Book Review

## NONFICTION

## *The Curtain*
A brilliant, delightful exploration of the novel—its history and its art—from one of the genre's most distinguished practitioners.

## *Testaments Betrayed*
> "A fascinating idiosyncratic meditation on the moral necessity of preserving the artist's work from destructive appraisal. . . . One reads this book to come into contact with one of the most stimulating minds of our era."
> —Boston Globe

## Other Books by Milan Kundura

### *The Art of the Novel*

> "Every novelist's work contains an implicit vision of the history of the novel, an idea of what the novel is. I have tried to express the idea of the novel that is inherent in my own novels."
> —MILAN KUNDERA

### *Encounter*

> "Cultivated, worldly, charming, and spirited.... Kundera's values are sane and humane; his impulses generous; his taste, overall, unimpeachable."
> —PHILLIP LOPATE, SAN FRANCISCO CHRONICLE

> "I can't imagine reading this book without being challenged and instructed, amused, amazed and aroused, and ultimately delighted."
> —JOHN SIMON, NEW YORK TIMES BOOK REVIEW

### *A Kidnapped West*

> "Offers insight into contemporary debates.... We should welcome the context Kundera gives for the struggles between Russia and Europe, and the plight of those caught between them. His defense of small languages, small cultures, and small nations feels pressing."
> —CLAIRE MESSUD, HARPER'S MAGAZINE

Other Books by Milan Kundura

"Kundera stands in the West as the representative Eastern European author of the second half of the 20th century—and the most celebrated Czech writer since Kafka."
—Wall Street Journal

**THEATER**

*Jacques and His Master*

Kundera's three-act stage adaptation of Diderot's eighteenth-century philosophical novel *Jacques le fataliste*.